Fact Finders®

The Story of Sanitation

WATER
ISN'T WASTED!

HOW DOES WATER
BECOME SAFE
TO DRINK?

by Riley Flynn

CAPSTONE PRESS
a capstone imprint

Fact Finder Books are published by Capstone Press,
1710 Roe Crest Drive, North Mankato, Minnesota 56003
www.mycapstone.com

Library of Congress Cataloging-in-Publication Data
Library of Congress Cataloging-in-Publication data is available on the Library of Congress website.

ISBN 978-1-5435-3112-1 (hardback)
ISBN 978-1-5435-3116-9 (paperback)
ISBN 978-1-5435-3120-6 (eBook PDF)

Editorial Credits
Anna Butzer, editor; Bobbie Nuytten, designer;
Morgan Walters, media researcher; Kris Wilfahrt, production specialist

Photo Credits
Capstone Press: Alison Theile, 18-19; Newscom: DISABILITYIMAGES\SCIENCE PHOTO LIBRARY, 12, Historica Graphica Collection Heritage Images, 11; Shutterstock: aleksander hunta, 20, brian legate, 22, Deyan Georgiev, 4, DiKiYaqua, 9, hedgehog94, 6, HUKEEHOM, (droplet) Cover, design element throughout, I WALL, (paper) design element throughout, JJJSINA, 25, johavel, 7, John1179, 24, Lisa S, 23, NatashaPhoto, 13, nito, 10, 28, OMMB, 16, Pablo Prat, 21, photopixel, (faucet) Cover, Robert Kneschke, 5, 29, SetSailPhoto, 27, Sukan Saythong, (filters) Cover, W.Tab, 14-15, 17, Yuri Samsonov, 1

Printed and bound in the United States
PA021

TABLE OF CONTENTS

CHAPTER 1
ALL ABOUT WATER

We use water for so many different things every day. We clean our houses and our bodies with it. We drink it and use it to flush our toilets. We water our crops and cook with it. Without enough clean water, our cities would be dirty and stinky. The world would be filled with dead plants and very thirsty people.

Farmers use large sprinkler systems to water crops.

We need water to live because our bodies are 60 percent water. Finding water and making it clean is important for everyone. **Purified** drinking water hasn't been around very long. For thousands of years, humans drank water that stank, tasted bad, and made them sick. In fact, in some countries, people still can't get clean drinking water.

HYDRATION IS HEALTHY

Water is the key to staying hydrated, or keeping a healthy amount of fluids in our bodies. When we sweat, our bodies lose water, so it's important to drink water when you're being active. But we also lose water from our bodies whenever we breathe or go to the bathroom. It's important to replace it by drinking water every day. To stay healthy, you need to drink about 10 cups (2.4 liters) of water a day.

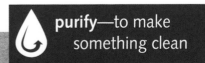

purify—to make something clean

People have worked hard to keep your drinking water safe. Thousands of engineers are working this very minute. They pipe water into treatment centers, purify it, and pipe it to your house. Now if you turn on the faucet, clean water comes out.

The United States uses more than 402 billion gallons (1.5 trillion liters) of water per day. That's more than any other country in the world. But it's less than it once was. Luckily, we are learning to use less water. That's pretty good because our population continues to grow. That means we have more people, but we use less water.

About 200 billion plastic water bottles are used around the world each year.

WATER, WATER, EVERYWHERE?

In the United States, the amount of water that people use has tripled since the 1950s. Water is being used faster than it can be replaced in some parts of the world. The chart below shows where people in the United States are using the most water.

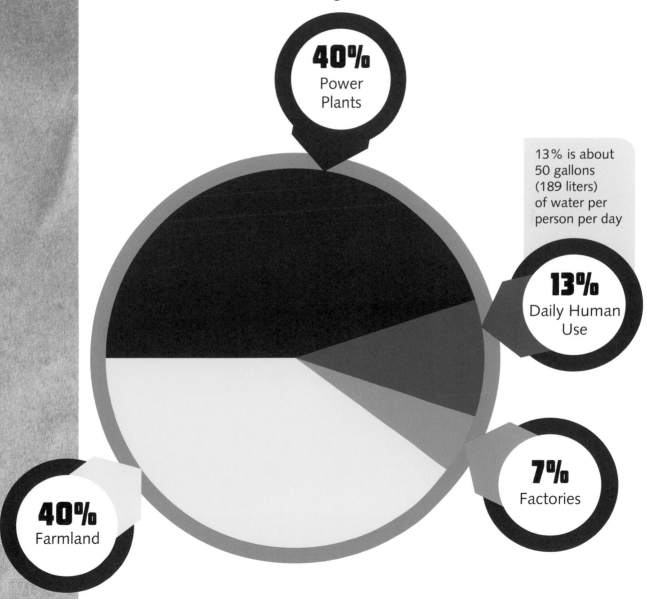

40%
Power Plants

13% is about 50 gallons (189 liters) of water per person per day

13%
Daily Human Use

40%
Farmland

7%
Factories

CHAPTER 2
THIRSTY PEOPLE IN HISTORY

In ancient times people didn't know about germs. But they did know that dirty water could make them sick. As the number of people on the planet grew, it became harder to bring clean water to everyone. So what did people do? They thought of new ways to clean water and bring it to people.

Intelligent Indians

In Ancient India, people didn't know what germs were. But they still found a way to keep from getting sick. Ancient Indians heated water until it boiled. Then they filtered it by pouring it through sand and gravel. Both of these techniques clean water. Boiling water kills germs, and filtering clears out other yucky stuff.

Boiling water kills germs and parasites. It is the safest method of purifying water.

CLEAN COINCIDENCE

Around 400 BC a Greek physician named Hippocrates discovered ways to improve drinking water. At this time the quality of water was determined by its smell, taste, and appearance. Hippocrates found that boiling water removed the bad smells and tastes. He didn't realize that it also removed germs that could cause diseases.

Roman Plumbing

Ancient Romans built **aqueducts** to bring water into their cities. These stone waterways transported water from one place to another. Romans didn't have electricity to power their aqueducts, so they used **gravity**.

The aqueducts started at the top of mountains. Streams flowing down the mountains poured into the aqueducts.

aqueduct—a large bridge built to carry water from a mountain into the valley

gravity—a force that pulls objects with mass together

At one point Rome had 11 aqueducts. The longest aqueduct was 59 miles (95 kilometers).

The aqueducts ran along, spilling water into wells and pipes. The water passed through clay and sand filters to clean it. Some of the water was piped into the homes of the emperor and other rich people. The rest went to public fountains, where common people could fill their buckets.

As time went on, the ideas of the ancient Indians and Romans disappeared. When wars broke out, large sections of the Roman aqueducts were ruined during attacks on Rome. After that, Romans would get their water from local rivers.

Once the Roman aqueducts were no longer usable, people used polluted, dirty river water.

CHAPTER 3

FROM STREAM TO STORAGE

We've learned a lot about cleaning water since ancient times. Scientists from many different fields have taught us about **bacteria** and bad chemicals. They've also discovered how to get rid of germs.

Today water is tested, treated, and cleaned so it's safe to drink. **Lab technicians** at water treatment centers have learned the best ways to clean water. Water goes through a series of steps to be cleaned.

FACT The most common steps in water treatment are coagulation, sedimentation, filtration, disinfection, and storage.

Lab technicians at water treatment plants make sure our drinking water is free of bacteria and waste.

Water is pumped from a water source and moved through pipes to a water treatment center. Then the first step in water treatment, **coagulation**, begins. Chemicals that act like magnets are added to the water. These chemicals make all the dirt particles in the water clump together, or coagulate.

This process was invented by Ancient Egyptians. Amazingly, after thousands of years, technicians use the same chemical the Egyptians used—**alum**. Technicians today add some other chemicals too, but alum is still the main ingredient.

bacteria—one-celled, microscopic living things that exist all around you and inside you

lab technician—a person who is trained in a specific technical process in a laboratory

coagulation—a process that cleans water by causing some liquids to turn to solids and sink to the bottom

alum—a type of crystal that helps purify water

Alum, or aluminum sulfate, is widely used for water treatment.

As the dirt clumps stick together, they become heavy and sink to the bottom of the water. This part of water treatment is called **sedimentation**. Then the clear water on top is pushed through a series of filters. These filters are made out of sand, gravel, or charcoal. They remove the smallest specks of dust, bacteria, and chemicals.

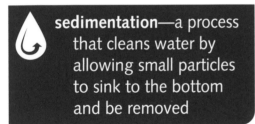

sedimentation—a process that cleans water by allowing small particles to sink to the bottom and be removed

Sedimentation tanks get a little help from gravity. The particles get heavy and sink to the bottom of the tank.

The Deal with Disinfection

The next step is disinfection. This process can be done in two different ways. Usually an **element** called **chlorine** is added to the water to kill any remaining germs. It is also used in swimming pools to keep bacteria from turning the water green.

Scientists know that chlorine breaks down into other chemicals that are harmful to fish. They think these same chemicals may not be good for people either. Some cities are now using **ultraviolet light** instead of chlorine in their water treatment facilities.

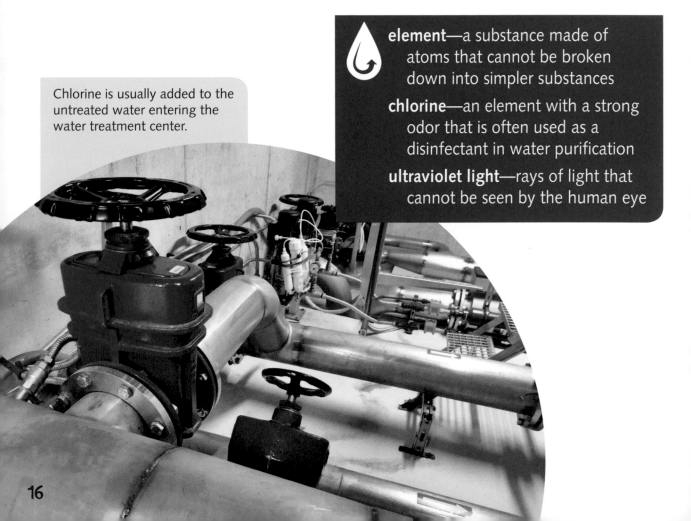

Chlorine is usually added to the untreated water entering the water treatment center.

element—a substance made of atoms that cannot be broken down into simpler substances

chlorine—an element with a strong odor that is often used as a disinfectant in water purification

ultraviolet light—rays of light that cannot be seen by the human eye

Ultraviolet light waves can be harmful and cause sunburns. But those same light waves can also kill germs that make us sick. Lastly, water goes into storage until people need to use it. You know that big water tower with your town's name on it? That's where clean water is stored. Cities also store water in underground holding tanks.

Water treatment centers use a minimum of three different filters to clean water.

The Treatment Train

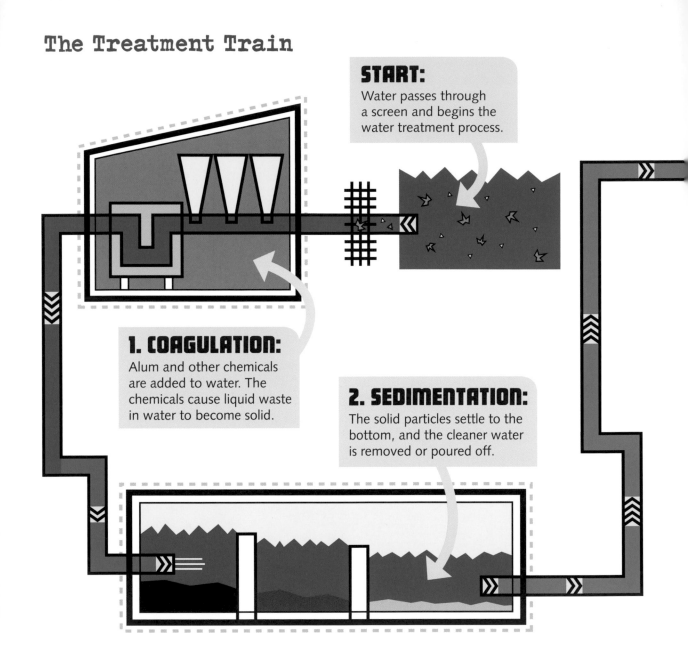

START:
Water passes through a screen and begins the water treatment process.

1. COAGULATION:
Alum and other chemicals are added to water. The chemicals cause liquid waste in water to become solid.

2. SEDIMENTATION:
The solid particles settle to the bottom, and the cleaner water is removed or poured off.

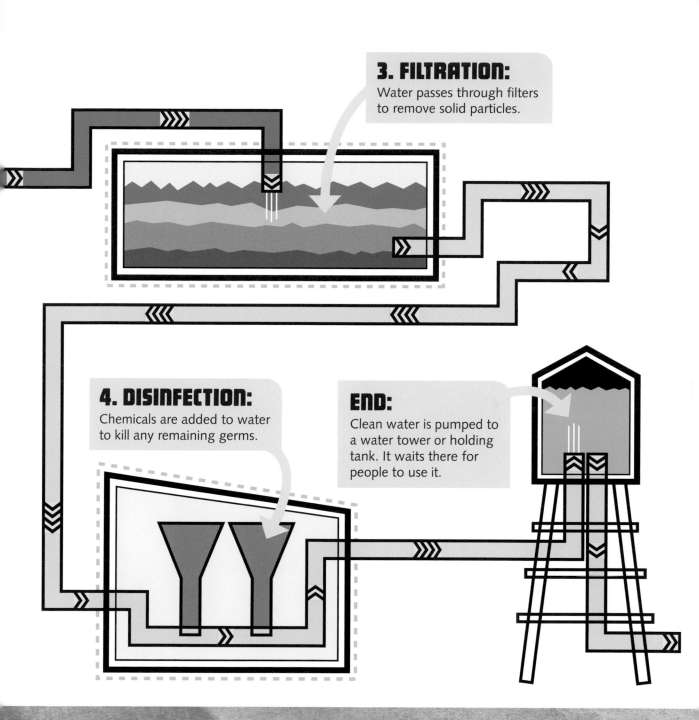

3. FILTRATION:
Water passes through filters to remove solid particles.

4. DISINFECTION:
Chemicals are added to water to kill any remaining germs.

END:
Clean water is pumped to a water tower or holding tank. It waits there for people to use it.

Where Does Water Come From?

People use two kinds of water—groundwater and surface water. Surface water comes from streams, river, lakes, and **reservoirs**. Groundwater is found underground.

Even water that looks clear and clean can have germs in it.

Groundwater is formed when water seeps into the ground and collects in **aquifers**. People dig wells to reach aquifers. Shallow wells are around 50 feet (15 meters) deep. Bigger wells can go down 1,000 feet (305 meters) or more. The deeper the well, the cleaner the water.

When water travels down that far, it passes through lots of sand, rock, and soil. These elements naturally filter the water. Unfortunately, you can't replace groundwater. Once an aquifer or a well is empty, there is no way to refill it.

Depending on where the water is coming from, it is treated, or cleaned, in different ways. But both surface water and groundwater can become **contaminated**.

Reservoirs are man-made bodies of water that are usually created in areas where there are not many lakes that are safe for drinking water needs.

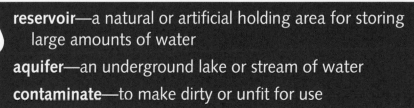

reservoir—a natural or artificial holding area for storing large amounts of water

aquifer—an underground lake or stream of water

contaminate—to make dirty or unfit for use

No matter where our water comes from, it is affected by what happens on the land around it. Sometimes, when it rains a lot, water can no longer soak into the ground. When this happens, the rainwater travels to a water source as **runoff**. The runoff picks up **pollutants** on its way to rivers, streams, and lakes. Some of these pollutants contaminate our water sources.

We all contribute to the contamination of our water. Most of the time we don't even realize that we're doing it. We contribute to water contamination if we use toxic cleaning products or forget to pick up our dog's poop!

A street water drainage pipe empties out into nature.

runoff—rain that is not absorbed by the soil

pollutant—a harmful material that can damage the environment

Contamination of our water sources can cause diseases. Sometimes a contaminated water source can become impossible to clean, and the source can't be used anymore. Polluted runoff is the number one cause of water quality problems today.

The amount of runoff water is even higher when there is heavy rain.

CHAPTER 4

PROTECTING OUR WATER

Did you know there are laws in place to help protect water? These laws protect water sources and help keep water clean. There are also laws that limit the amount of water we can use on our lawns and gardens. Because water is easy to access, some people don't think about how much they are using.

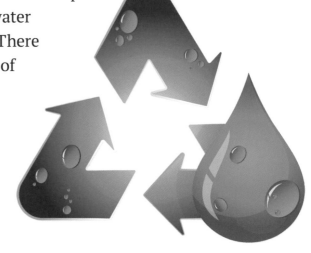

WATER WITH RULES

In 1970 the Environmental Protection Agency (EPA) was created to protect human health and the environment. In 1974 the Safe Water Drinking Act was put in place to protect the public drinking water in the United States. Laws and agencies similar to these are put in place across the world so everyone can have safe drinking water.

Water is a limited resource, so **conserving** it is very important. There are many simple ways to save water. We can turn the water off while brushing our teeth, take shorter showers, and make sure none of our faucets are leaking.

FACT Ask your parents to help you test for leaks by placing a drop of food coloring in your toilet tank. If the color shows up in the toilet bowl without flushing, you have a leak!

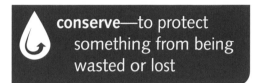

conserve—to protect something from being wasted or lost

Americans drink about 1 billion gallons (3.8 billion liters) of tap water every day.

City planners and engineers work hard to find the cleanest water sources possible. They make sure that factories aren't dumping waste into reservoirs. They clean the water from sewer systems before pumping it back into rivers. They test for chemicals and poisons before the water even gets to the treatment plant. No matter how clean a water source looks, water is not safe to drink until it has been treated.

We all need water to survive. That's why engineers are filtering, cleaning, and pumping water right now. Many cities have thousands of gallons of water in underground holding tanks or water towers. It's just waiting for someone to turn on the tap and have a drink.

Water towers are often made of concrete, steel, or brick.

FACT Water towers are used to hold water for the town or community they are near. Water towers hold about a day's worth of water. For most water towers, that is about 1 million gallons (3.8 million liters).

TIMELINE

312 BC

The first Roman aqueduct is built.

1804

Paisley, Scotland becomes the first city in the world to provide filtered water for the entire city.

1965

The Water Quality Act is created in the U.S., and states are ordered to make rules for the quality of waterways crossing over state boundaries.

1746

The first widely used water filter was created. It was made of wool, sponges, and charcoal.

1908

Water treatment plants in America start using chlorine to treat water.

300 BC   **1500**   **1900**

1980

The United Nations declares the start of the International Drinking Water Decade. They hope to bring attention and support for clean water worldwide.

1970

The Environmental Protection Agency (EPA) is established in the U.S.

1974

Congress passes the Safe Drinking Water Act to help protect America's drinking water.

2009

The EPA updates the number of contaminants that are not allowed to be in our drinking water or only very small amounts can be found in our drinking water.

1970

2000

GLOSSARY

alum (AL-uhm)—a type of crystal that helps purify water

aqueduct (AK-wuh-duhkt)—a large bridge built to carry water from a mountain into the valley

aquifer (AK-wuh-fuhr)—an underground lake or stream of water

bacteria (bak-TEER-ee-uh)—one-celled, microscopic living things that exist all around you and inside you; many bacteria are useful, but some cause disease

chlorine (KLOR-een)—an element with a strong odor that is often used as a disinfectant in water purification

coagulation (koh-ag-yuh-LAY-shun)—a process that cleans water by causing some liquids to turn to solids and sink to the bottom

conserve (kuhn-SURV)—to protect something from being wasted or lost

contaminate (kuhn-TA-muh-nayt)—to make dirty or unfit for use

element (EL-uh-muhnt)—a substance made of atoms that cannot be broken down into simpler substances

gravity (GRAV-uh-tee)—a force that pulls objects with mass together; gravity pulls objects down toward the center of the earth

lab technician (LAB tek-NIH-shun)—a person who is trained in a specific technical process in a laboratory

pollutant (puh-LOOT-uhnt)—a harmful material that can damage the environment

purify (PYOOR-uh-fye)—to make something clean

reservoir (REZ-ur-vwar)—a natural or artificial holding area for storing large amounts of water

(Glossary continued)

runoff (ruhn-AWF)—rain that is not absorbed by the soil

sedimentation (sed-uh-muhn-TAY-shun)—a process that cleans water by allowing small particles to sink to the bottom and be removed

ultraviolet light (uhl-truh-VYE-uh-lit LITE)—rays of light that cannot be seen by the human eye

READ MORE

Enz, Tammy. *Liquid Planet: Exploring Water on Earth with Science Projects*. Discover Earth Science. North Mankato, Minn.: Capstone Press, 2015.

Feinstein Stephen. *Drying Up: Running Out of Water.* The End of Life as We Know It. New York: Enslow Publishing, 2016.

INTERNET SITES

FactHound offers a safe, fun way to find Internet sites related to this book. All of the sites on FactHound have been researched by our staff.

Here's all you do:

Visit *www.facthound.com*

Type in this code: 9781543531121

 Check out projects, games and lots more at **www.capstonekids.com**

CRITICAL THINKING QUESTIONS

1. What are some ways we can help keep our water sources clean?

2. Why is it important that every person on Earth has access to clean water?

3. Look at the infographic on page 7. What are some ways you can reduce the amount of water you use?

INDEX